BEING LOVED

Being Loved
A Handbook for Spiritual Growth
by Blake Steele

Copyright © 2003 Scandinavia Publishing House
Drejervej 11-21, DK 2400 Copenhagen NV, Denmark
Tel.: (45) 35310330   Fax: (45) 35310334   E-Mail: jvo@scanpublishing.dk
Text copyright © 2003 Blake Steele
Photo copyright © 2003 Blake Steele
Design by Ben Alex

Second Edition
Printed in Singapore
ISBN 87 7247 267 7

Spiritual Vision Series
by Blake Steele

A God to Desire
Being Loved
Radical Forgiveness
Creative Compassion

SPIRITUAL VISION SERIES

BEING LOVED

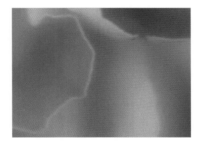

A HANDBOOK FOR SPIRITUAL GROWTH

WORDS AND PHOTOGRAPHY
BY BLAKE STEELE

scandinavia

4

This book series is specifically designed to inspire and guide you towards spiritual healing and transformation. It gives you tools to take spiritual reality from a mental understanding to a heart experience where all the good things happen.

Being Loved focuses on an essential key to spiritual growth, that only to the degree we allow ourselves to be loved and blessed by God will we have the capacity to share His Love with our world. To receive unconditional love makes us joyous, openhearted, and able to love and accept others with a grace of life that is infectious.

It is my heartfelt wish that this little book becomes a warm companion and helpful tool for you on your journey towards spiritual freedom.

BLAKE STEELE

AS THE FATHER HAS LOVED ME, I HAVE
LOVED YOU. LIVE IN MY LOVE. JOHN 15:9

In this saying Jesus revealed his heart. He received God's Love
with a wide-open spirit, and from the fullness of being loved
poured Love out into the world.

6

AND WE HAVE KNOWN AND HAVE BELIEVED
THE LOVE THAT GOD HAS FOR US. I JOHN 4:16

Jesus knew that he was lavishly loved: He drank it in, breathed it
and bathed in it. To him, Love was a living power—the divine
source of Life that birthed him and nurtured his soul into loving.

known, that we might be
gh his entire being.

his being said yes, yes, yes!
e in his bones. Every cell of
aneously loved us from his
n the clear light of his
is ecstatic delight to set

GOD IS LOVE... 1 JOHN 4:16

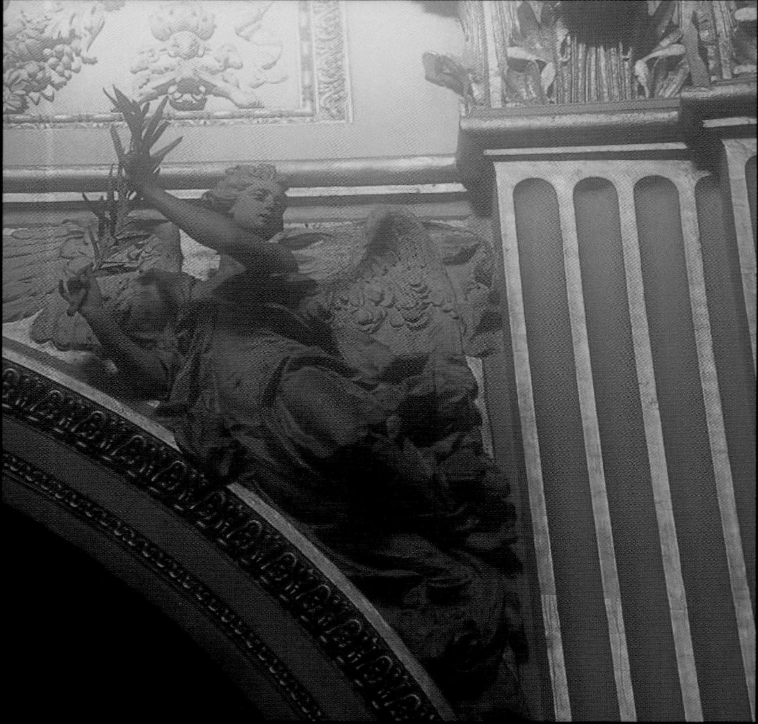

THE LORD IS COMPASSIONATE
AND GRACIOUS... Ps 103:8

God is compassionate Love. He has created all things in the overflow of His joyous nature to share. Utterly pure in His nature, profoundly simple and free, blessing and healing all who receive Him—God loves because God is infinite Love.

In Jesus we see how Love can pour freely out of the Being of God. The power of God's healing presence was his proof of God—not arguments or theological surmising. Through Christ the God of compassion and grace breaks out into the world.

Love pours out to create Love.
Nothing more. Nothing more.

13

14

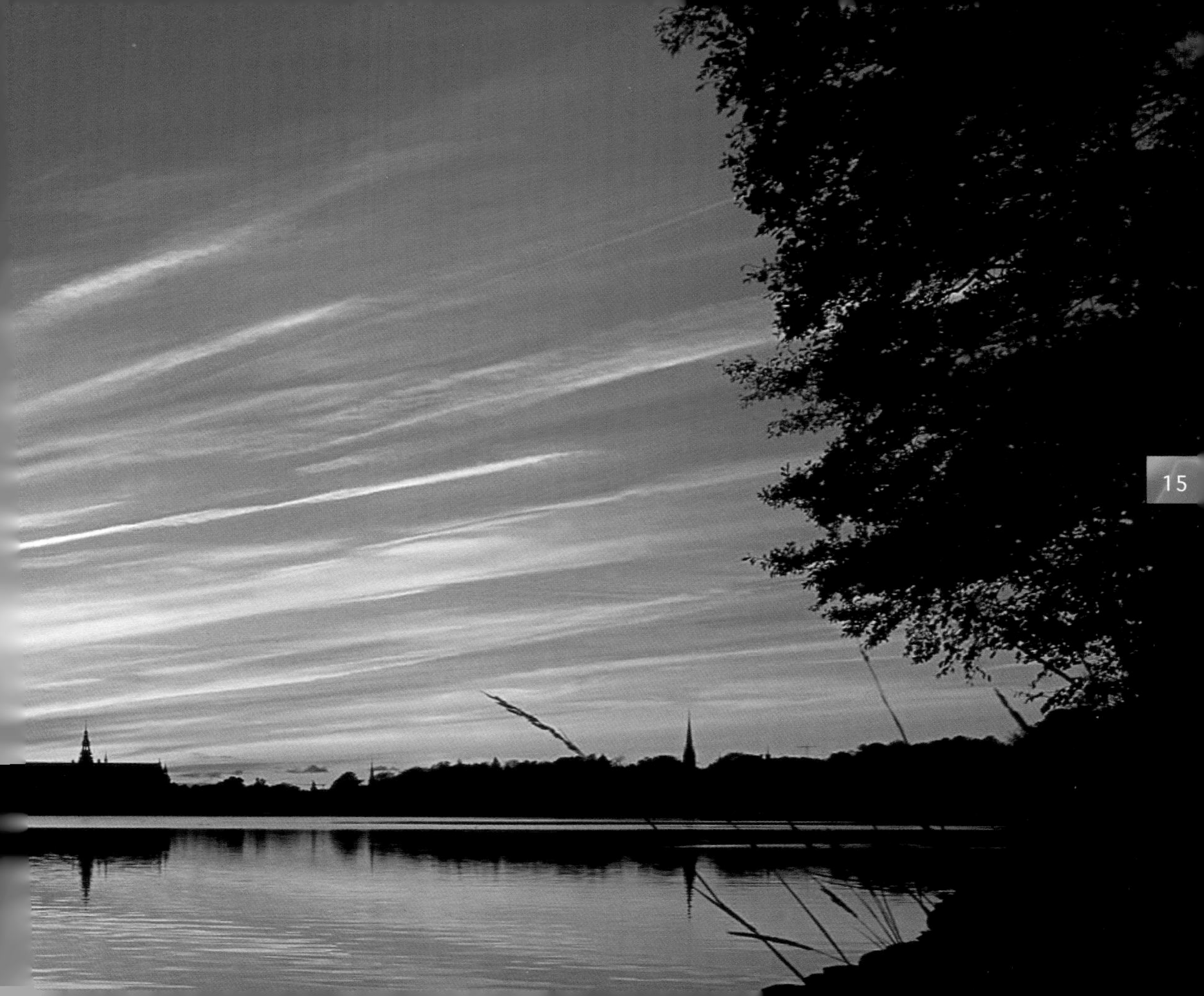

Christ is Love. The beauty of God shone from his face. When
people saw Jesus they fell in love with him. Why else would they
drop everything and follow him? The work he saw the Father
doing, he did. He touched blind eyes and they opened; he put his
fingers in deaf ears and they heard. Jesus healed because God is
healing Love—the great spiritual reality that can set us free.

The Spirit of Love poured through Jesus,
and flowed and flamed and flooded.
It was an artesian well bubbling
and billowing from Christ's innermost being;
a clear stream flowing from his belly—
pouring forth a free existence
from his freedom of infinite goodness.

16

I AM THE WAY, THE TRUTH AND THE LIFE. John 14:6

Jesus did not give us a philosophy about life, but fully embodied the way to become our truest, most unique selves. He is our way. He is pure Love loving us completely. To know His Love is to know the Father as a fountain of Life.

CHRIST, THE POWER AND WISDOM OF GOD. I Cor 1:24

As God's self-expressive Word, the entire Universe exists within Christ. He is the heart and soul, the molder and meaning of life. His power and wisdom is revealed from the infinite whirl of stars right down to the radiance of photons and quarks. And Christ became a man to reveal God in man and man made free in Love— for this is God's purpose for everything.

Christ is the living wisdom of God.
Who can tame the lighter of the sun?
Who can confine he who forms mountains
and makes rivers run? Yet, he comes
like a lamb, and lies down in our wounded souls.
Like a lover, he kisses us with warm breath
in a word of Love.

22

AND WE HAVE SEEN AND TESTIFY THAT THE FATHER HAS SENT HIS SON TO BE THE SAVIOR OF THE WORLD. I JOHN 4:14

Christ poured out his life to save the world he passionately loves. By his sacrifice all moral debt was cancelled, all punishment for wrong was paid in full and we are welcomed home in freely offered forgiveness as the unearnable gift of his grace. (Ephesians 2:8)

Forgiveness is full release. We are forgiven by pure Love for not living Love, sharing Love, being Love—for being selfish and blind and hurtful. We are forgiven completely so that we might learn the lessons completely, then arise and shine in the beauty of his Love and overflow with Life's goodness into the world.

For God so loved the world
He gave His only Son... John 3:16

The Gospel is a love story, a revelation from the heart of Creation. The life of Christ is the greatest tale of sacrificial Love ever told. And it's true—transforming the heavens, able to recreate your heart and mine. For our hearts were made for Love and will not find wholeness apart from that Love who created stars, the oceans and earth, you and I, and all things, for Love, Love, nothing but Love. To be transformed by the Spirit of Love is the highest purpose of being, the essential meaning of existence.

Simply live in Love for Love—
for the beauty of it,
for the joy of loving.

24

26

27

YOU ARE PRECIOUS IN MY SIGHT,
AND I LOVE YOU... ISAIAH 43:4

28

Being loved is the process of welcoming His Love into every part of our being, an experiential journey of transformation into Love's nature of loving. It is growing freer in the life-affirming nature of Love that has no conditions or requirements other than that we receive it—for only to the degree we allow ourselves to be loved and blessed by God will we have the capacity and freedom to share a transformative Love with our world.

When my daughter Rebekah was a baby she was shy and quietly observant, surrounded by exuberant, active children. One morning, while sitting in her highchair eating oatmeal, a lot more got on her face than in her mouth. We all laughed and told her how cute she was and she obviously soaked up the attention. So the next morning she turned an entire bowl of oatmeal upside down on her head and smiled happily as it drooled down her face and over her ears. I'll always remember the look of innocent joy in her eyes.

We all seek attention; we thrive on it: for attention is awareness and awareness is the presence of Life. God is pure awareness, infinitely tender, loving presence. Being loved is welcoming God's loving presence into our bodies and souls. It is waking up to know that God is above us, below us, around us, within us, loving us completely.

31

Let your mind settle on one intent:
to let Love blow through the wide open
window of your heart, blinds cast back,
silk curtains billowing—riding easy
on delicate breaths of breeze.
An open heart resists all the world's reason
to pull the blinds.

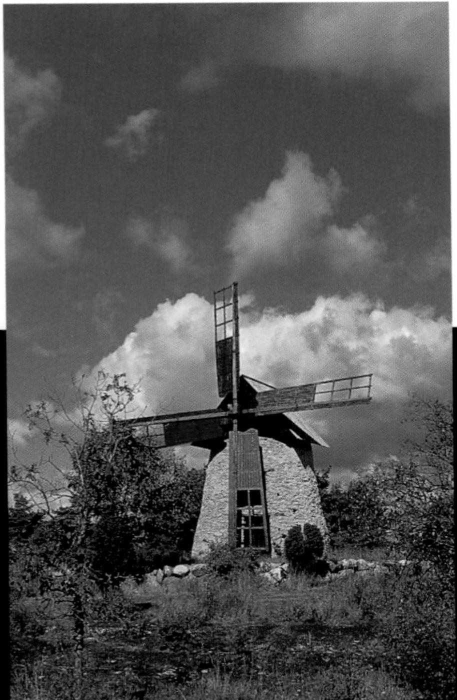

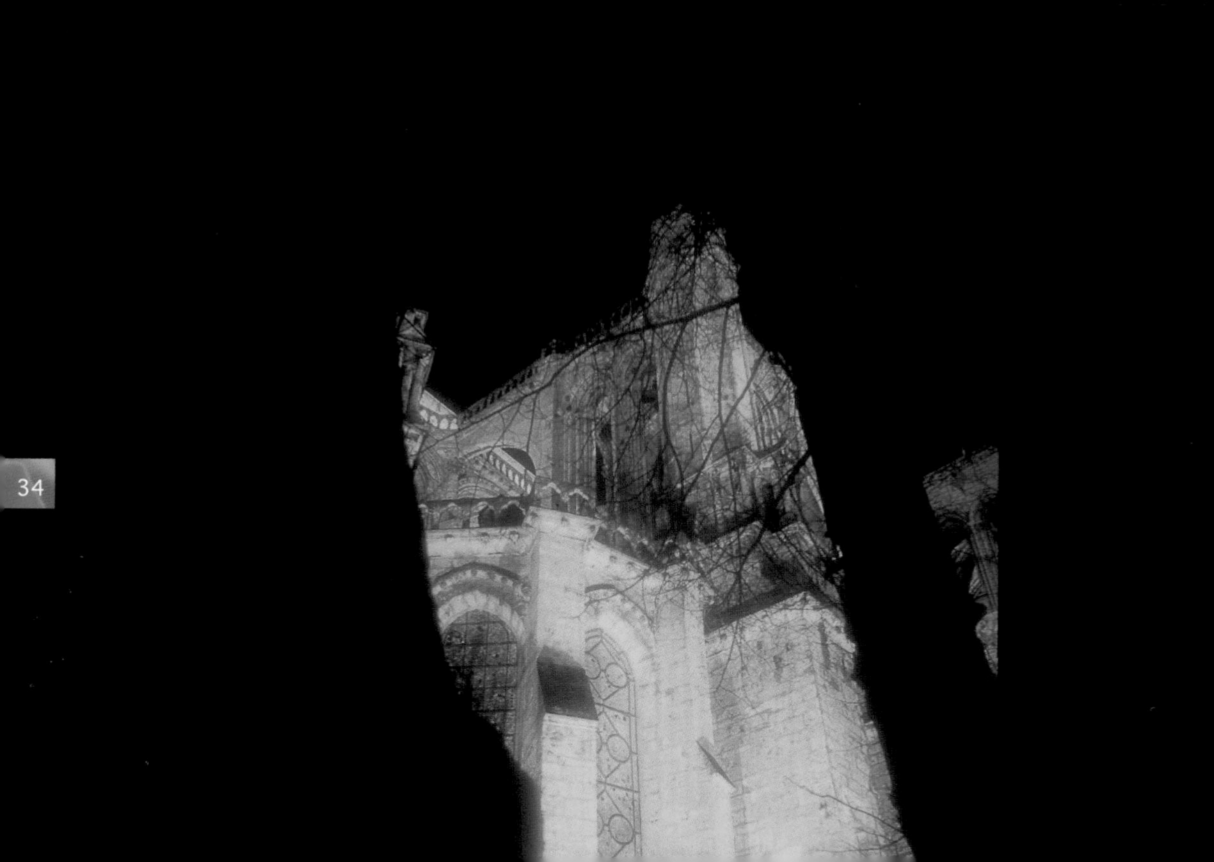

WHOEVER DOES NOT LOVE DOES NOT KNOW
GOD, BECAUSE GOD IS LOVE. I JOHN 4:8

A bird knows exactly what it is to be a bird. A fish expresses its essential fishiness. But we so easily miss the mark of our being, hit the wrong target, forget there is a target, and miss the point of it all, which is Love.

35

...LOVE IS THE FULFILLMENT
OF THE LAW. ROM 13:10

We need to be loved. Of all human needs, it is the greatest. When we are starved for Love life goes wrong. It is the failure of people to nourish each other with Love that is the sin of the world, the sin that casts shadows in every heart.

HE IS WOOING YOU FROM THE JAWS
OF DISTRESS TO A SPACIOUS PLACE
FREE FROM RESTRICTION... JOB 36:16

The roots of guilt, shame, anger and blame, all drink from one dark river: a deep spiritual ache of grief caused by isolation from the freedom and inspiration of Love. And so, cut off from what is ultimately real, we are ashamed and grieved concerning our crippling insecurity and secret life of pain. The defense mechanisms we build at first to protect ourselves become negative unconscious forces restricting and imprisoning us, causing us to further wound ourselves and others.

And so, sin goes on, suffocating our highest potential, distorting our soul's expression of life.

IN ALL THEIR DISTRESS, HE TOO
WAS DISTRESSED... Is 63:9

As light streams through the pupil of the eye, so Love pours
through an open heart. But when we are hurt, to open our heart
goes contrary to a deep instinct to protect ourselves. We are afraid
of Love's tender vulnerabilities that could increase our pain. And
so the open pupil of our soul constricts, and we shut out the Spirit
of Love that would heal us.

Yet, if in our pain we ache for Love and grasp after it with
desperate neediness, we only push it further from us—and so
our need increases. To be free, this vicious cycle must be broken.

Beyond the harshness of a wounded world,
deep in the shadows, God hovered,
weeping with you in your weeping.
Though your innocent dreams
were disfigured by calloused cruelty,
God still dreamt of you:
beautiful, washed in clean rivers,
growing through all suffering
to be your truest, most beautiful self,
healing in the goodness of His Love
that makes stars shine,
hearts beat, and reveals again
the beauty of the world.

42

I WILL GIVE YOU A NEW HEART AND PUT A NEW SPIRIT WITHIN YOU... EZE 36:26

The most passionate purpose of Christ is for us to receive a new heart that is open to God, beautiful with Love, blessed with God's blessing that makes us a fountain of blessing in the world.

What is required above all things is letting God love us just as we are so we can grow into all we can be. This saves us from trying to save ourselves and is the way of grace.

44

46

My daughter Amber was a very independent child who wanted to do everything herself. One day we heard a desperate cry from the upstairs bathroom, "Help me, somebody..." We found her stuck in the toilet with only her head, arms and little feet sticking above the bowl. Her eyes were wide open with fear. "Help me," she cried again in a wavering voice. Her strong, independent spirit had momentarily vanished. All her struggles to free herself had only wedged her in tighter. She was terrified she might be flushed.

Many of us have to come to a similar place in our lives—in the toilet bowl, helpless, afraid of being flushed—before we allow ourselves to be helped by someone greater than us. It is when we finally realize that any more struggling will only make things worse that we are ready to call out and allow someone wiser and stronger than us to lift us out of our predicament. It is at that moment we discover the meaning of grace.

BY GRACE YOU ARE SAVED, THROUGH
FAITH... IT IS THE GIFT OF GOD... EPH 2:8

Grace is God's free gift of liberation. It is Christ pouring out his life for us in complete forgiveness without the slightest hint of shame or blame. It is God warmly welcoming us home to the healing of His Love. It is rivers of His Spirit flowing through our hearts. It is the atmosphere of freedom that allows Love's new creation.

There is no way to earn grace. We can't barter for it, beg for it, or make a deal. Grace is as freely given as sunshine, being pure Love and selfless, full of Life and joyously free. Accepting grace freely is the only relationship we can have with it—for the only condition God puts on grace is that we put no conditions on it. Faith is not a condition to receive His grace. It is simply a hand opening to accept the gift.

49

GOD HAS POURED OUT HIS LOVE INTO
OUR HEARTS BY THE HOLY SPIRIT
WHOM HE HAS GIVEN US. ROM 5:5

By grace God pours His Love into our heart through the gift of His Spirit. No matter what our life as been, we can ask for His Spirit to wash us with freshness—for His Spirit is the pure freedom of grace.

His Spirit is the kindness and acceptance our soul needs in order to heal. His Love can flow right into our deepest hurts, our darkest shame, to renew our hearts in a freedom that is deliciously desirable and joyously infectious. In Christ, the doors are thrown wide open. Whoever is willing can receive the blessings of His Love.

Life's great purpose is letting God love you into freely loving.

Christ's way is as simple as flowers.
It is the way of trust in His Love—
the way of the heart.

52

Trust is not the mind trying hard to believe. It is the mind that creates divergents, excuses, symbolic representations it mistakes for reality, and veils of every kind. But the moment we let go and simply open our heart, trust is born—for faith flows by His Spirit through our heart into our blood and bones. It is our heart that is capable of moving right into Love, for Love is a spontaneous reality the heart was designed to receive.

53

IN QUIETNESS AND TRUST IS
YOUR STRENGTH. Is 30:15

One day a fly caught one of its toes in a spider's web. 'It's no problem,' he thought, 'I'll just do a few quick maneuvers and be out of here before the owner arrives.' So he twisted, and a wing was caught; he dipped, and was stuck by his belly; he spun, and another leg was caught. The more he struggled the more hopelessly trapped he became.

Whenever we struggle to accept Love, we only enmesh ourselves more deeply in our insecure and needy nature. But letting go of struggle is an effortless effort: it is like a deep sigh, a fist unclenching, a simple yes to grace that opens our heart.

How many years have you gone through your house
shutting the windows because of the storms outside,
when all along, the storms were in your basement?
The purple clouds, the thundering billows,
the rattlesnake strike of lightning that wounds,
rattled your doors and made you shudder.

Don't you want to forget all that enclosure
and run from window to window
and door to door,
throwing open everything to the sky
shouting, here I am,
here I am,
now,
here am I!

58

Trust in His grace is saying yes to His great Yes of us, and no to our No of Him. To deny our denial of Love is to realize we are no longer this resistance, but are someone else, hidden in Christ and already free. Faith in His grace allows His eternal Yes of Love to arise like a sun in the hidden depths of our heart.

"Lovers alone wear sunlight." —E. E. CUMMINGS

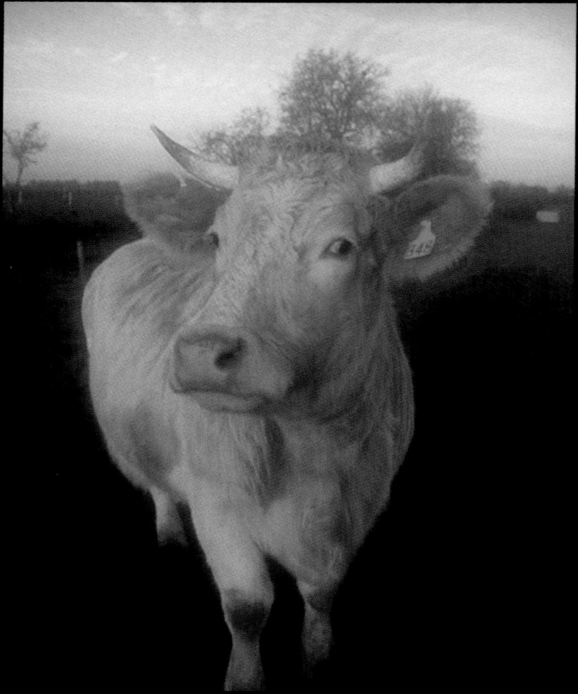

IT IS GOOD TO GIVE THANKS
TO THE LORD... Ps 92:1

Saying Yes! to His Love fills our hearts with thankfulness. And
thankfulness is the essence of joy.

Try this: for the next minute simply appreciate everything that God
freely gives to us all. Thank God for the sun and moon, the sky
and beauty of the earth. Thank Him for birds and animals. Give
thanks for the gifts of air and water and your every breath and
heart beat. Then give thanks for every person you love. When you
are done, see if you don't feel happier and lighter.

"Love has reasons which reason cannot understand." —BLAISE PASCAL

Now thank God for loving you completely, just as you are.
See for yourself how thankfulness releases trust in His Love.

With an attitude of trust and gratitude we can safely open every
door in our hearts to let His Love dispel our fear, dissolve our
grief, sooth every pain, give us a whole new way to understand
our lives.

Because God is love, God loves me.
Like the sun loves the earth, God loves me.
Like the sea loves a stream, God loves me.
Of course I am loved. I am loved!
Because God is love, God loves me.

> DO NOT LEAN ON YOUR OWN
> UNDERSTANDING; BUT IN ALL
> YOUR WAYS ACKNOWLEDGE
> HIM. PROVERBS 3:5,6

God doesn't see us as we see ourselves. All negative interpretations and beliefs concerning our selves that block His desire to bless us with Love are a hindrance. To heal, our minds need to harmonize with His way of understanding us. Of course, we can't fully grasp how the Maker of the Universe understands our lives—but we can acknowledge this: if we understood ourselves as He does we would be luminous and free.

The moment we accept this is true, a whole new way of understanding opens to us. The self-judgments that have supported our separate existence from God's Love are meaningless. All that matters to God is Love's new creation.

66

DO NOT JUDGE AND YOU WILL NOT BE JUDGED; DON'T
CONDEMN AND YOU WON'T BE CONDEMNED, FORGIVE
AND YOU WILL BE FORGIVEN... FOR IN THE MEASURE
YOU MEASURE IT WILL BE MEASURED TO YOU. LUKE 6:37,38

We must surrender our right to judge ourselves, for we have never
seen ourselves correctly until we have seen through the eyes of
God's compassionate Love. His purpose is to set us free to grow,
to learn, to let negativity go. Forgiveness is the release that can
transform all the experiences of our life into compassion.

For Love's sake, yield your present understanding of your life to
Christ who perfectly understands you. Your whole life is designed
to teach you the value and wisdom of Love. Open your heart to
understand your life-experience more compassionately and see
what happens—for as you harmonize your heart with God's
purpose, His Light flows in.

HOW BEAUTIFUL YOU ARE, MY DARLING, HOW
BEAUTIFUL YOU ARE! YOUR EYES ARE LIKE
DOVES BEHIND YOUR VEIL... SONG OF SONGS 4:1

God sees us now as we eternally shall be. This is His creative faith
for us, the faith by which we can truly live. From Him pours the
power and freedom to become as beautiful and full of Life as His
Love envisions us. Catch a glimpse of your eternal face in the
mirror of His Love. There you are open, and innocent, and free.

How beautiful you are in God, for in Christ everything is beautiful
with Love. How new, how fresh, how bright, how alive: just
beyond all mentally created veils, misdirections, and misplaced
hopes, your great soul is waiting—hidden in him. There you are,
silent, watching, ready to arise.

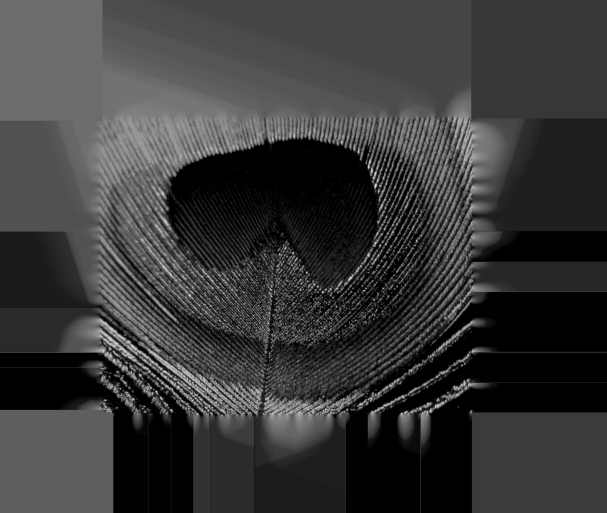

Free to love our self in loving God,
harmony flows.
Happiness is the natural flow of God.
The innocent love of the Lamb
flows through our innocent intent to be open.
We open our heart and our heart sings
with the clean river's silvery songs.
Love flows, loving us, loving our souls,
our opening bodies.
Love sings its innocent songs in every cell.

74

Once there was a simple monk whom the Lord granted a special grace of visitation. Every night, when the brother was alone in his cell, the Lord would come and stand before him. Then the monk would fall on his face and cover his eyes, for he was afraid that he would see in his Lord's eyes an accusation regarding some hidden sin or a demand that he was not willing to fulfill. Finally, one night the Lord spoke to him.

"Brother Armond, why don't you look at my face".

"Lord, I am afraid of seeing my own unworthiness," the monk replied.

"Look at me," the Lord said, very gently.

The monk summoned his courage and looked up. There was no accusation or demand, just all the Love of heaven flowing through Christ's eyes into his heart.

That was the last night the Lord came, but from that time on, Brother Armond became known as, The Shining One.

ALL THAT COUNTS IN CHRIST
IS A NEW CREATION... GAL 6:15

God loves us, every part of us, in ways we do not love ourselves. And as we open to His Love flowing through us, it can dissolve the self-judgments and grief that nourish selfish resistance and restore to joyous innocence all that sin warped and threatened to destroy.

God loves your face. Do you? God loves your hands and feet. Do you? God loves your body. Do you? God has forgiven you completely for your most painful failings, for the moment of your greatest shame. Have you? Each opinion we hold regarding our self that is not luminous with His Love must be transformed.

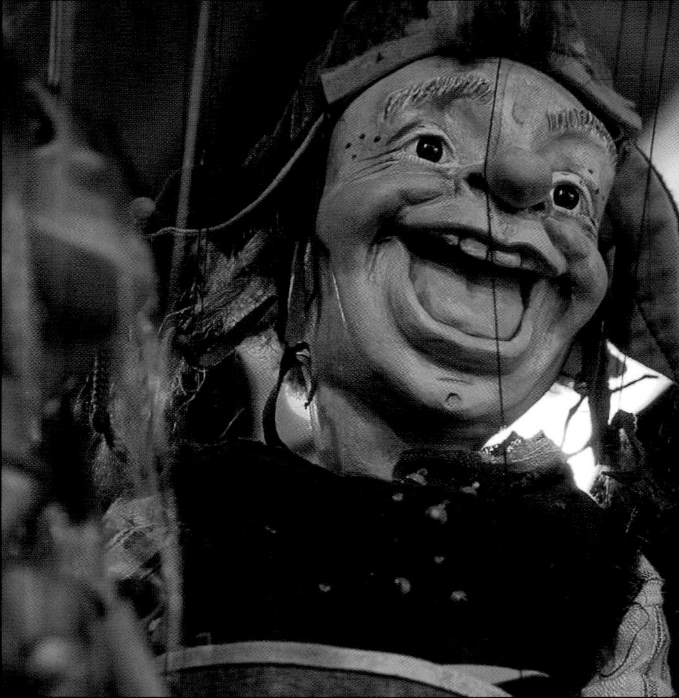

Letting God love you is the key of spiritual healing. It is a process of dissolving away false beliefs and self-judgment until your heart no longer negates His Love. If you are always critical of yourself, how will people ever feel God Loving you? And if they don't sense the wonder of His Love for you, why should they desire Him?

Being loved means being very kind and patient with your self, and radically forgiving your self in His grace. It means welcoming every wounded part of you home to His Love. That's what the child of God in you needs in order to express itself at its highest potential.

God is loving me for I am learning to allow it:
to experience what has always been true.
God is so free! And I am free!
Where did this huge, robust laughter come from?

LOVE YOUR NEIGHBOR AS YOU
LOVE YOUR SELF. MARK 12:31

Some people mistake loving your self for self-absorption: but these are often the ones who are unhappy servants of the God of joy. Self-absorption is rooted in insecurity and a sense of separation from God. But yielding our hearts to harmonize with God's Love for us is just the opposite. It unites us fully with God and makes us secure in the healing nature of His Love.

All my life I sought to please myself.
In pleasing God I am cherished.
All my life I sought to please others.
In pleasing God I am loved.
And how do I please God, you may ask?
I accept I am cherished,
I run around in His love.

WE LOVE BECAUSE HE FIRST LOVED US. I JOHN 4:19

God wants to love you, right up through every layer of your being and all your deepest needs until your heart, mind, and every cell of your body are singing yes to Love. Then the Love you share with your family or friends, or your neighbor next door, will have an impact far beyond the words you say or even what you do. It's who we are that opens people's hearts to what we have to share—and the glow of a soul being loved is unmistakable.

God passionately loves you, as He loves me.
Happiness is knowing this with a child-like heart.

IF WE LOVE ONE ANOTHER, GOD LIVES IN US
AND HIS LOVE IS MADE COMPLETE IN US I JOHN 4:12

God pours out Love freely from His infinite tenderness. Drink
Love in. Soak it up. You cannot be too blessed! As your
receptivity grows your life will flow with the wonder of His Life
and the inspiration that makes being loved infectious. It is His
Spirit that unites us with others, heals us, and opens our eyes to
the beauty of Christ in us—this wonder of Love.

THIS IS LOVE: NOT THAT WE LOVED GOD, BUT THAT HE LOVED US... I JOHN 1:10

The way of being loved is the way of the heart. It begins with our open receptivity to trust in His grace and moves through the transformation of our hearts until His Love freely spills through our lives.

This really is a spiritual universe, full of God's glory. When Love opens our hearts, it opens our eyes, revealing God's presence everywhere, loving us, calling us to His freedom. We just don't know how beautiful life can be until we wake up in His Love.

All things exist to be blessed with Love. Open your heart—you are loved so much more than you know.

90

When I was young, I was extremely critical of myself. Then, when I became a follower of Christ, it seemed that God was very hard on me as well. It was words of warning and judgment, not grace, which often jumped out at me from Scripture. And the more I tried to be like Jesus, the worst things got.

After much suffering and failure I woke up to realize that it wasn't God who was being so hard on me—it was my own self-critical heart. I saw that I was trying so hard to be good because my wounded self was deeply afraid of being rejected by God. When I realized that Christ not only died to liberate me from the fear of death, but also from all judgment—especially my own—I found the courage to fire my own relentless inner judge. This changed my life completely. The meaning of grace burst fully upon my soul, and with it the freedom of God began to be revealed. Now the more I allow Him to love me the more I find myself simply being a blessing as my old, wounded self melts away in His Love. And the more I move from self-effort to effortless trust, the more effortlessly He moves.

I don't believe this book would be complete without mentioning the relationship of Love to death and grief. Most of us have been touched by suffering and death—powerful experiences that shape our lives. The shock of death and its finality can seem almost surreal. Someone we love is torn from the fabric of our soul and the gaping hole that is left howls.

It is not possible to love others in this world without eventually suffering the grief of loss.

Though suffering and death are inevitable, bitterness is not. Love is a powerful antidote to the bitterness, blame and self-pity that often arise from the shock of death. By opening our pain fully to His Love in the midst of our grief our capacity for compassion is deepened when our suffering is done.

In Christ, death is a door into luminous worlds. Through Him, God transforms all sorrow into joy by reuniting those who love each other in deathless beauty. This is His eternal promise that brings ultimate meaning to it all.

Meditations on Being Loved

Along with prayer and worship, meditation and waiting on God are ancient Biblical ways to open our hearts to God's love.

The Hebrew words for *meditation* mean to murmur, ponder deeply and imagine; and in the Greek to revolve a matter around in the mind with care.

In the New Testament, Paul prays that through the Spirit, the eyes of your heart may be enlightened, that you might know the hope of your calling and riches of His glory in us. (Ephesians 1:18) In Greek this phrase, *the eyes of your heart being enlightened,* means to gaze at your mind's focused thought or at imaginative imagery that is shining with God's light. This is a simple and powerful New Testament way to meditate and wait on God. It is one of the ways first century Christians used to let Christ live fully in their hearts and be formed within them.

Our imagination is our God-given creative capacity. Imaginative imagery is the language of the deep heart and is just as real to it as imagery from the physical senses. Just daydream the realities of God you cannot see with your physical eyes; let the eyes of your heart see and God's Spirit will fill your heart with His Love and beauty, the riches of His glory in us.

The Hebrew words translated *waiting on God* mean to interweave your being with God, to watch with hope, to know nothing and be astonished, to stop, to gather yourself and wait in silence. Meditation naturally flows into waiting on God, communing together in a deep stillness of peace that is beyond understanding.

Here are ten meditations to help you weave your heart into God's heart, to see His presence with an imaginative gaze that allows you to experience the riches of the glory of His Love—and allows Him to love you completely.

You don't need to spend much time with a meditation: quality of time and regular repetition are what have a powerful effect in the heart. Do one, and then let go. Rise up. Live your life fully knowing that He is at work deep within you, healing things, making new connections and shifting things around. These meditations make space for Him to freely do His work of Love in you.

1. Open to Him when He comes and knocks... Luke 12:36

Christ is always standing at the door of our heart; always knocking with every nudge towards love and kindness, with every experience of life that teaches us how loveless selfishness just doesn't work. The doorknob is on our side of the door. By simply making the choice to let Him love us, the door opens.

Imagine a door in the center of your chest. Simply open the door with a heart-felt *Yes* because you want your heart wide-open to His Love. Imagine the door opening and the bright light of His Love shining through and flooding your entire being. Let Christ gently embrace you within and melt all resistance to His Love. Let go. Surrender. Relax into His arms. Allow His Love to flow into whatever resistance you may feel. Whisper to Him whatever comes to your mind or sit in silence and simply savor His presence. Be loved.

Prayer: *Lord, thank you for creating in me an open heart that knows you are always here, always now, with arms wide open, eternal Love loving me.*

2. And He breathed on them saying, "Receive the Holy Spirit." John 21,22

The Hebrew word *Ruah* means spirit, breath, wind... In ancient Middle Eastern spirituality, breath has always been linked with spirit as Jesus does here. For example, Job mentions the breath of God in our nostrils. (Job 27:3) Opening to His Love can be as simple as breathing.

Breathe in slowly and deeply and sense the breath moving into your lungs. This is a physical expression of the open, spacious, breath of God moving freely into your spirit.

Relax deeper into the feeling of space inside your chest. God is right here, in open space, wholly transcendent yet intimately present in all Creation. God is intimately present in you. Feel your breath and draw it into your heart. Imagine your heart as a free, open space within you. From this space, God loves you constantly. Through this space, the Holy Spirit pours. Make friends with open spaciousness. Meet God there.

3. GOD OVER ALL, THROUGH ALL, IN ALL. EPH 4:6

Take a deep breath. Now simply sense what is in your body. Is it pain and tension, or stillness and peace?

God is in you, just beyond these sensations. He is an infinite ocean of Love, here and now, in which every molecule of your body exists. If your body and the entire world faded away, God would remain, loving you. With a simple yes of faith, acknowledge His timeless presence. Imagine all sensation fading away and rest your entire body for a moment in His stillness. Now drink it into your sensations. Feel His healing smile. Allow God to love you completely.

Prayer: God above me; God below me; God around me; God through me. God beyond all; God in all; God loving me; God loving all You have made. I yield to be loved and blessed without limits. Amen.

4. THE LORD SETS THE PRISONERS FREE. Ps 146:7-8

Imagine yourself as a blind child crying in a prison cell. A thorn is sticking in your heart and the pain won't stop. You are chained to two starving people. One is filled with fear; the other is anxious and needy, grasping for whatever comes its way. The prison door opens and Christ comes in. He pulls the thorn out of your heart and your chains fall off. Your eyes open and you hug Jesus with joy and laughter.

Next, see yourself as you are now, standing in front of Jesus on the cross. The needy person and the fearful person are standing next to you. See them drawn as if by a strong magnet into the body of Christ. As He dies, they die.

Now imagine the risen Lord coming and hugging you. A bright light shines out of His heart. Let yourself melt right into Him and see the light of His heart unite fully with yours. See your heart shining, and your whole self free and happy—filled with His Love.

5. IF I DO NOT WASH YOU, YOU HAVE NO PART WITH ME. JOHN 13:8

I love this bright dawn of joy, this flood of Love washing me,
the warm heart of Christ pressed against my heart.

Let the Son of God love and cherish you. Imagine Him washing your feet with a sponge that is full of His Spirit. Let Him wash your whole body with His Love. Everywhere the sponge passes, your body is washed innocent and clean. Open every part of your body and being to Him. Hold nothing back. Hear Him whisper, *I have washed you, and you are Mine.* Imagine a warm flood of Love pouring through your body from head to toes.

Prayer: *Yes, yes! Thank you Lord for cleansing every cell in my body. I wash in your Spirit until my whole being sings in your freshness.*

6. UNTIL... THE SHADOWS FLEE AWAY. SONG OF SONGS 4:6

The one who is infinitely loved is wearing clouds for clothes.
Let them melt in sunshine and blow away in God's winds.

Feel for any cold, gray, inner clouds that separate you from the bright presence of Christ. Name them if you can and let yourself feel them fully. See them filling you and surrounding your body. Now imagine yourself stepping into a shower. Turn on the tap and take a shower in liquid sunshine. Imagine the clouds melting away in the warmth of His Love splashing all over you. Imagine the sparkling water flowing right through you, washing you inside from head to toe, washing the clouds out the bottoms of your feet and down the drain. Step out of the shower. Imagine His winds blowing upon you with freshness and freedom.

Prayer: O Lord, thank you for melting away the clouds of my heart by your Spirit. I bring all of my life, sunshine and shadows, into your Love.

7. YOU ARE GOD'S HOUSE, AND THE SPIRIT OF GOD LIVES IN YOU. I COR 3:16

God loves each of us with infinite Love and understanding. Though our experience of His Love is limited by our capacity to receive it, we can exercise and expand our capacity.

Feel your toes. The atoms in your toes are spinning in the infinite sea of God. God is loving your toes. Imagine your toes shining with God's light. Wiggle them and love them. Feel your feet and legs. God is limitless Love loving them. Imagine them shining with His Love.

Step by step, open all your body to His light. When you feel a resistance, it is an old self-judgment or a negative emotion that needs to be washed away. Imagine God flowing right into that resistive feeling to embrace it with forgiveness and dissolve it with Love. Imagine the innocence of Christ filling every muscle, every organ, and every cell. You are His home and He is your Life.

Prayer: Lord, flow through my imaginative faith with power. May all my body sing, Yes! *in your Light.*

8. BUT WHILE HE WAS STILL A LONG WAY OFF, HIS FATHER SAW HIM, AND FELT COMPASSION AND RAN AND EMBRACED HIM AND KISSED HIM. LUKE 15:20

Imagine yourself as the prodigal son in Jesus' parable. Let any sense you have of separation, neediness or fear fill the dirty and despondent child who is returning home.

Imagine your father running to you and kissing you again and again. Let the father's servants take off your dirty rags. See yourself being clothed in royal robes. Feel the acceptance, the welcoming Love, your father's joy that you have come home.

Embrace everything within you that you have been trying to get rid of, hide, or push away. Imagine every shamed part of you entering the feast of life.

See yourself standing in your father's house with your arms opened wide. Over you doors are opening and sunlight steams through. Below you doors are opening. To the right and the left, bright doors are opening. In your heart a door is opening. Your heart is shining like a star.

9. I PRAISE YOU FATHER... THAT YOU HAVE HIDDEN THESE THINGS FROM THE WISE AND INTELLIGENT AND REVEALED THEM UNTO BABES... MATT 11:25

When the heart opens completely,
receiving God's Love is simpler than breathing.

Sit quietly.
Slowly lift up your hands as a gesture saying,
Lord, here is my heart.
Sense your heart.
Breathe His Love into your heart.
Breathe in open space.
Say, *Holy Spirit flow through my heart.*
Breathe out His Love.
Breathe in Love; breathe out Love.
Do it again and again.
The way of the heart is simple.
A child can find it.

10. DRINK AND IMBIBE DEEPLY, O LOVERS. SONG OF SONGS 5:1

Imagine yourself at a feast.
A beautiful angel smiles
and puts a large golden cup in front of you.
On the cup is written the word, *Grace*.
Take a sip of God's grace.
Imagine that it is the best taste you
have ever experienced.
Take big gulps of it and feel it fill you
with warm peace and Love.
Rest for a few moments sensing God's
complete acceptance of you,
within and without.
Whisper, *Because You love me, I love You.*

Do this 3 times a day for one week.
Keep on doing it forever.

A Final Thought

TRULY I SAY TO YOU, WHOEVER DOES NOT RECEIVE THE KINGDOM OF GOD LIKE A CHILD SHALL NOT ENTER IT AT ALL. MARK 10:15

Please don't be fooled by the simplicity of these exercises. It is spiritually true that images and emotions are intimately connected in the deep heart. Don't try to change your emotions directly because will power, more emotion, or reason are not the right tools. Imaginative imagery is. Try this for yourself with emotions and negative self-criticisms that oppress you. Let yourself feel fully what is in you. It is vital that you don't try to push away or bury a negative thing in your heart. Rather connect it to imaginative imagery from one of these meditations, a scripture or imagery God personally gives you. As you learn to just let the emotion be and freely change the image you will experience how the emotion also changes. This shift of focus from trying to control emotions to transforming the imagery that represents it gives you power over what is in your deep heart. You never need to feel helpless again. This transformative principle is another amazing gift of His Love.

Blake Steele is one of God's vagabonds on earth, traveling to do creative work and share God's abundant love through personal encounters and workshops. A versatile artist, he has written over 2,000 poems, a novel, children's stories, is a lyricist for choral pieces and a photographer. In this book series he shares his vision, wisdom and awe for God through photography and poetic writing.

For personal contact visit: *www.beingloved.net*

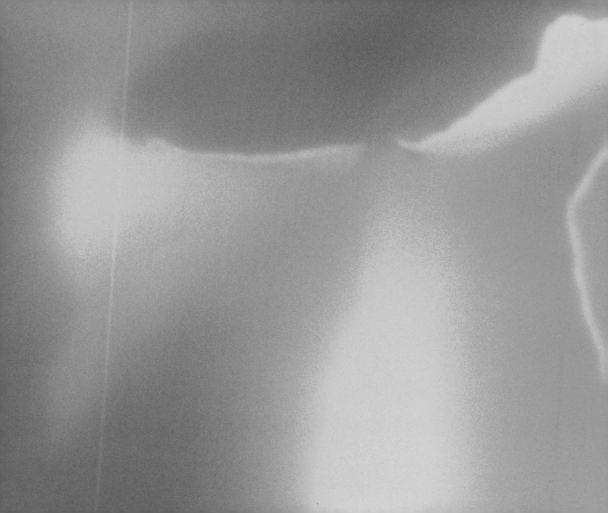